SUPERSTARS of PRO FOOTBALL

ANTONIO GATES

Ian Kimmich

Ypsilanti District Library
5577 Whittaker Road
Ypsilanti, MI 48197

Mason Crest Publishers

Produced by OTTN Publishing in association with
21st Century Publishing and Communications, Inc.

Copyright © 2009 by Mason Crest Publishers. All rights reserved. No part of this publication may be reproduced or transmitted in any form or by any means, electronic or mechanical, including photocopying, recording, taping, or any information storage and retrieval system, without permission from the publisher.

MASON CREST PUBLISHERS INC.
370 Reed Road
Broomall, Pennsylvania 19008
(866) MCP-BOOK (toll free)
www.masoncrest.com

Printed in the United States of America.

First Printing

9 8 7 6 5 4 3 2 1

Library of Congress Cataloging-in-Publication Data

Kimmich, Ian.
   Antonio Gates / Ian Kimmich.
     p. cm. — (Superstars of pro football)
ISBN 978-1-4222-0553-2 (hardcover) — ISBN 978-1-4222-0823-6 (pbk.)
 1. Gates, Antonio, 1980– —Juvenile literature. 2. Football players—United States—Biography—Juvenile literature. 3. San Diego Chargers (Football team)—Juvenile literature. I. Title.
GV939.G38K56 2008
796.332092—dc22
  [B]   2008024192

Publisher's note:
All quotations in this book come from original sources, and contain the spelling and grammatical inconsistencies of the original text.

◀◀ CROSS-CURRENTS ▶▶

In the ebb and flow of the currents of life we are each influenced by many people, places, and events that we directly experience or have learned about. Throughout the chapters of this book you will come across CROSS-CURRENTS reference bubbles. These bubbles direct you to a CROSS-CURRENTS section in the back of the book that contains fascinating and informative sidebars and related pictures. Go on. ▶▶

CONTENTS

1. **All Pro, All the Time** — 4
2. **The Pigskin and the Hoop** — 10
3. **From Rookie to Pro Bowler** — 16
4. **Big Money, Big Games** — 26
5. **Charging Ahead** — 36

Cross-Currents — 46
Chronology — 56
Accomplishments & Awards — 57
Further Reading & Internet Resources — 58
Glossary — 59
Notes — 60
Index — 62
Picture Credits — 64
About the Author — 64

ALL PRO, ALL THE TIME

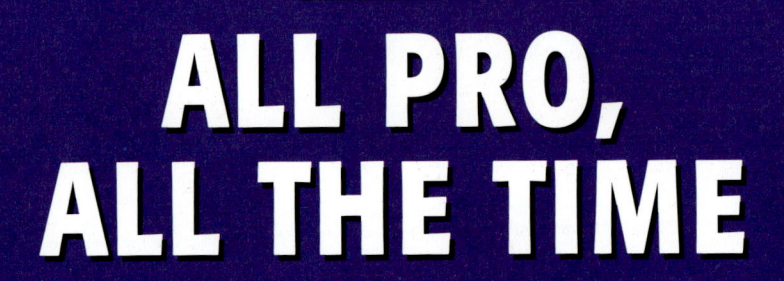

The San Diego Chargers broke from the huddle and positioned themselves on the line of scrimmage. It was a few minutes into the second quarter of the team's October 28, 2007, game against the Houston Texans. The Chargers were leading, 14–3, and had the ball on their opponent's 49-yard line.

The Texan defenders shifted, trying to match up with San Diego's receivers, running backs, and tight end. One Charger the Texans watched was number 85, Antonio Gates. Antonio, the Chargers' six-foot, four-inch, 260-pound tight end, had lined up outside the usual spot for a tight end. He was positioning himself like a receiver—a big receiver.

All Pro, All the Time 5

After just five seasons in the National Football League, Antonio Gates has emerged as one of the league's best tight ends. A former star basketball player, Antonio uses his size, leaping ability, and good hands to make big plays.

ANTONIO GATES

The ball was **snapped**. The **quarterback** took a few steps backward, scanning the field for threats and for open Chargers. Antonio moved faster than his defenders, working his way across the field. The football left the quarterback's hand, spiraling toward Antonio. A defender closed in, but Antonio blocked him out, snatched the ball as it whizzed through the air, and took off up the field.

> **CROSS-CURRENTS**
> To understand more about the role of the tight end in a team's offense, check out "A Tight End's Universe." Go to page 46.

The tight end's powerful strides tore up the yards, and he blew past would-be tacklers. It was as if the defenders were watching the game from the bleachers with the fans—they could not even touch number 85. After putting 31 yards and 11 Houston defenders behind him, Antonio Gates stepped into the end zone for a **touchdown**. Listening to the cheers of his home crowd, Antonio smiled. He had just given his team a convincing lead. It was his second touchdown of the game and his fifth of the season.

Top Tight End

In 2007, Antonio Gates had been in the National Football League (NFL) for five years. He was already thought of as one of the best tight ends to ever play the position.

New England Patriots coach Bill Belichick, who is regarded as one of the top coaches in the NFL, said of Antonio,

> **He has enough quickness to separate and size to separate against smaller defenders like [defensive backs]. He can go out jump them for the ball. You can pretty much put the ball anywhere around him. He's got great timing and judgment.**

While Antonio's size and strength are not exceptional for a tight end—most men who play the position are tall, strong, and heavy—his speed, agility, reflexes, and **hands** are what truly set him apart. When he first entered the league, Antonio surprised everyone but the best-informed **scouts** with the way he ran routes, caught the ball, and picked up yardage after each catch. In the NFL, all players are fast and strong. It takes great skills to gain yards after a catch.

All Pro, All the Time

"Antonio forces teams to put their best cover guy on him," explains teammate Roman Oben. "He's too big for safeties and too fast for linebackers. He's talented enough to make a good cornerback look bad."

With his speed and power, Antonio has the skills to make great plays on the football field.

In 2005, Chargers quarterback Drew Brees said about his favorite target,

"He's actually kind of quiet. He doesn't say a lot. He just works and is competitive. Very competitive."

ANTONIO GATES

Antonio's first five years in the NFL were all spent with the San Diego Chargers, and his years were all spent well. Aside from his first season, in which he caught 24 passes and scored two touchdowns, Antonio performed each year in a way most professional football players can only dream of.

In 2007, Antonio earned his fourth **consecutive** Pro Bowl selection. Of about 2,000 players in the league, only the best go to the Pro Bowl. For a fifth-year player to have been selected for the Pro Bowl game four times in a row is incredibly rare.

In his first five seasons, Antonio racked up 340 receptions, or catches, and gained 4,362 yards. He averaged nearly 13 yards per catch, and 56.6 receiving yards per game. The 43 touchdowns Antonio has scored ranked him 21st among active players and 141st in NFL history.

CROSS-CURRENTS
Read "The Pro Bowl Story" to learn more about this annual all-star game for NFL players. Go to page 46.

In Antonio's first five seasons in the NFL, he was chosen to play in the Pro Bowl at Aloha Stadium in Hawaii four times. Antonio decided not to play in the game in 2008 because of a foot injury.

Powerhouse Package Deal

Antonio has helped change the way coaches, scouts, media, and fans view the duties of other players at his position. His performance has helped raise expectations for how tight ends should get open, catch the ball, and—most importantly—score. His four straight Pro Bowl team selections indicate his importance to the game.

Antonio Gates cares about more than just being a great individual player. He appreciates his team and his fans, and he works hard to put the Chargers in a position to win games, especially big ones. When asked about his feelings about all the praise and attention he was receiving for his outstanding abilities, Antonio said,

> "At the end of the year, I'll get a chance to enjoy my personal success. Right now, I just want to do all I can to contribute to this team and this offense."

Over and over again, Antonio has proven his value to his team. In the five years Antonio has been with San Diego, the **franchise** has won 50 out of 80 games. In the five years before Antonio joined the team, the Chargers won just 27. Antonio and a new generation of San Diego Chargers—including star running back LaDainian Tomlinson and quarterback Philip Rivers—are helping make the Chargers into an NFL powerhouse.

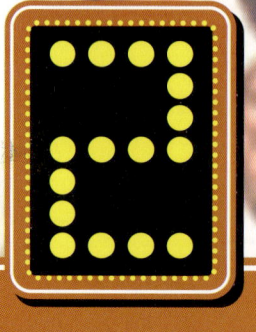

THE PIGSKIN AND THE HOOP

On June 18, 1980, Antonio D. Gates was born on the west side of Detroit, Michigan. Detroit was neither the safest of cities nor the easiest place to grow up, but Antonio found basketball courts and schoolyards in which to play sports. He played every sport he could, and he quickly dominated schoolyard ball.

Antonio's family was very important to him when he was growing up. Later in life he said,

"My family had the biggest impact on me. Outside of them, I would say society as a whole influenced me the most. I can't really point to one person as to why

The Pigskin and the Hoop   11

COULD SAN DIEGO BE AMERICA'S SMARTEST CITY?

SAN DIEGO
MAGA...

TOP SCHOOLS
How Our Elementary and Middle Schools Score

The Chargers' Winning Formula Off the Field

Fall Fashions with an Urban Appeal

Elder Abuse: An Old Story with a New Ending

SEPTEMBER 2007
$4.95US

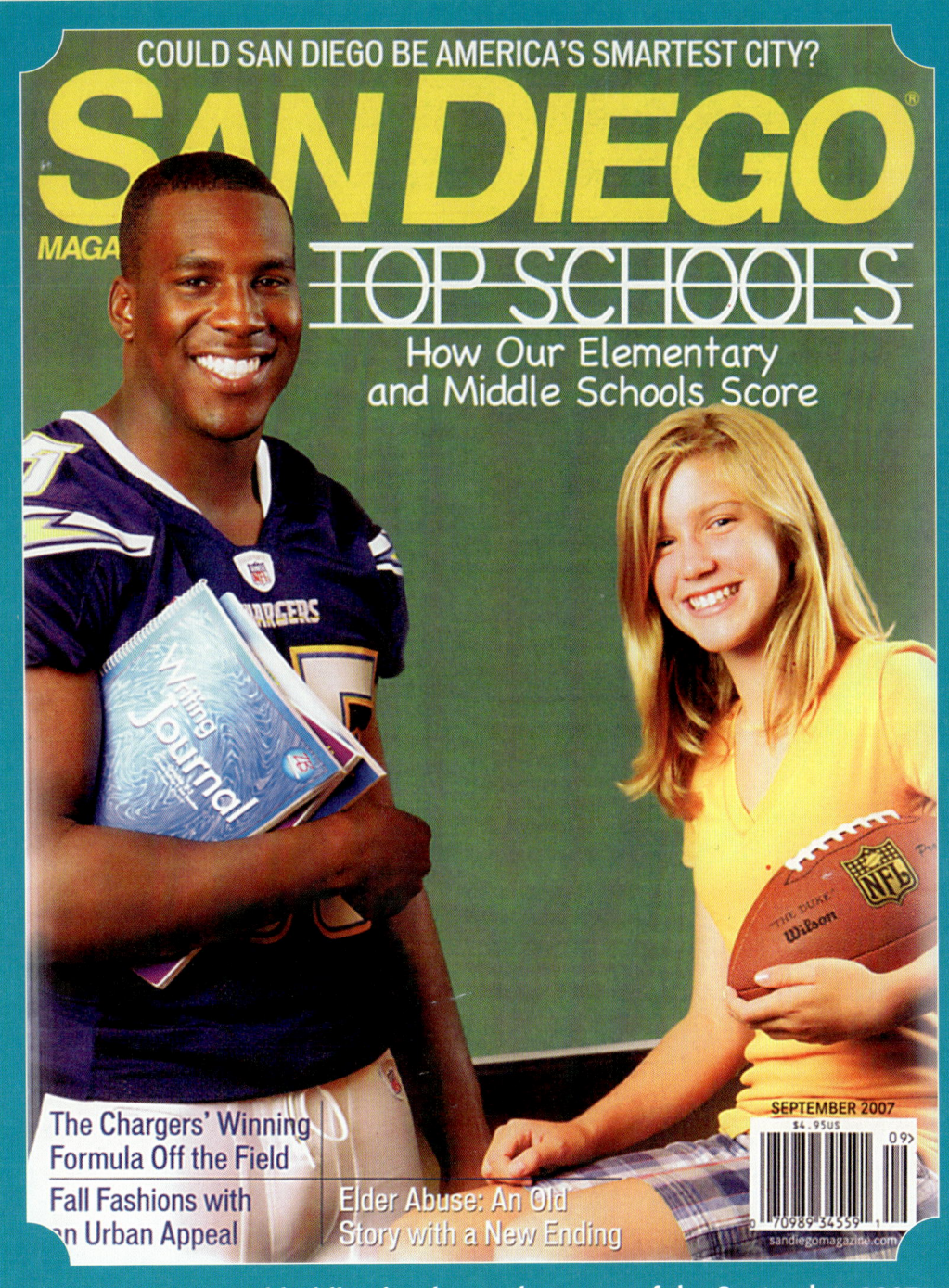

Antonio is pictured holding books on the cover of the September 2007 issue of *San Diego Magazine*. When Antonio was in school, his poor grades almost derailed his dreams of playing professional sports.

ANTONIO GATES

> **I did certain things. I wanted to do something that was different so I could stand out. I was in love with sports, and I wanted to become a professional athlete to separate myself from everybody else."**

Finding His Place

Antonio got an early taste of sports glory at Central High School, in Detroit. On the basketball team, he starred as a **power forward.** On the football team, he played both tight end and linebacker. Although high school tight ends usually block for other players, Antonio's main role on his football team was to catch passes. Antonio was so

At Detroit's Central High School, Antonio Gates was the heart of his team's offense and played linebacker on defense. "High school football in Detroit was not easy at all," Antonio later said. "There were talented players everywhere."

The Pigskin and the Hoop

talented that he was a standout athlete in both sports. However, he was not interested in school, and his grades suffered because of his focus on athletics.

After leading his team to the Class A Michigan State Championships as a senior, Antonio graduated from Central High with First-Team All-State honors in both football and basketball. His domination on the gridiron and the hardcourt earned him college scholarship offers. Antonio chose to attend Michigan State University because Nick Saban, the football coach, promised Antonio he could try out for the basketball team as well as play for the football team. Most other schools wanted him to pick just one sport.

When he got to Michigan State, however, Antonio faced a big problem. Under the rules of the NCAA (National Collegiate Athletic Association), all student-athletes have to keep their grades up to be allowed to play. Because Antonio's grades were not good enough, he had to sit out for his freshman football season. In addition, Saban told Antonio he could not try out for the Michigan State basketball team. Antonio was angry. Not focusing on schoolwork was threatening his sports dreams. By the end of his first semester, Antonio chose to transfer out of Michigan State instead of working to improve his situation there. Years later, Antonio admitted that he regretted leaving Saban's team:

> **"I was young; 17 years old. I was into basketball, having won many accolades in that sport. And, with him, it was kind of like somebody telling me I couldn't do it. I just didn't want to take no for an answer then."**

Antonio transferred to Eastern Michigan University, where he played 18 games for the basketball team in the 1999–2000 season. Antonio played well but, again, he had problems with school and lost his place on the team. To improve his performance in school, Antonio transferred, first to College of the Sequoias, in Visalia, California, and then to Dearborn Community College, in Dearborn, Michigan. After his break from college sports, Antonio transferred again, this time to Kent State University, in Kent, Ohio.

Antonio stayed at Kent State for his junior and senior years, and he gave the Kent State basketball program everything he had. Even

ANTONIO GATES

though he was small for a power forward—most are six feet, nine inches or taller—he was named to the All–Mid-America Conference (MAC) team at that position both years he played with the Kent State Golden Flashes. In his senior year, Antonio averaged 20.6 points and 7.7 rebounds per game, led his team to the MAC championship game, was the runner-up MAC Player of the Year, and received an All-America Honorable Mention.

The highlight of Antonio's college basketball career actually came during his first season with Kent State, when he led the Golden Flashes to the MAC championship. Their 30 wins set a school record for the most victories in a season. Although they were an **underdog** in the 2002 NCAA Division I Men's Basketball Championship tournament, also known as March Madness, the Golden Flashes made it to the Elite Eight round—the quarterfinals of the tournament.

CROSS-CURRENTS
To find out more about the biggest college basketball tournament held each year, read "NCAA March Madness." Go to page 48.

Hoop Dreams Meet Reality

As graduation neared, Antonio heard from coaches and **scouts** that he was too small to play power forward as a professional. Football teams, however, were more interested in him:

> "Midway through my senior season in college, all these NFL scouts were coming through to watch my basketball games. I was wondering why they kept showing up. It didn't matter how well I played. I could score 50 points in a game, and they would still be telling me I looked like I could be a good tight end. I was wondering what I had to do to convince people I was a basketball player."

CROSS-CURRENTS
For more information on how free agents like Antonio enter the NFL, read "Undrafted and Free." Go to page 49.

He did not want to leave basketball, but Antonio knew a good opportunity when he saw one, so he invited NFL teams to come watch him perform football drills. The San Diego Chargers immediately liked what they saw. Antonio presented a large target to quarterbacks. He

The Pigskin and the Hoop

"[T]he exposure I got by helping Kent State to the Elite Eight gave [NFL teams] a chance to see how well I moved," Antonio later explained. "I worked out for eight or nine teams, but the Chargers picked me up."

had good hands and quick feet, and his time on the basketball court had given him great skill at one-on-one matchups and blocking other players from the ball. On April 28, 2003, Antonio signed a two-year deal with the Chargers as an undrafted free agent. He soon headed for San Diego to join his new team.

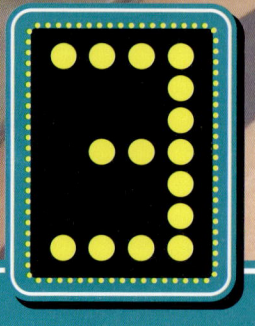

FROM ROOKIE TO PRO BOWLER

In August of 2003, Antonio arrived in sunny San Diego. This city is located on the California coast, just north of the border with Mexico. The warm, dry weather and excellent wave conditions make San Diego a skateboarding and surfing center, but once locals enter Qualcomm Stadium, they become wild for the Bolts—their nickname for the San Diego Chargers.

Warming Up

The addition of Antonio Gates to the team was the talk of the town in the summer and early fall of 2003. After watching Antonio practice, Marty Schottenheimer (the Chargers' coach at the time) said,

From Rookie to Pro Bowler

> **"It became clear real fast that he was going to make the team. You can't find that type of athleticism in men his size."**

Schottenheimer was right. Other players, especially defenders, were having a lot of trouble matching up against Antonio. Although he was criticized for what some people saw as mediocre blocking skills, Antonio appeared to be the ultimate tight end package. He was, however, a rookie and unlikely to get much playing time because the team had more experienced tight ends. Also, Antonio's coaches wanted to be careful about using him too much, because he had not played in a competitive football game since high school. He needed time to adjust to the speed and intensity of NFL games.

The San Diego Chargers play on their home field, Qualcomm Stadium. In the three seasons before Antonio arrived, San Diego had been a bad team, winning just 14 games while losing 34.

ANTONIO GATES

Antonio jogs onto the field during San Diego's training camp, July 2003. Antonio's first regular-season NFL appearance came on September 14, 2003. Two weeks later, he caught his first pass, for 17 yards, in a game against the Oakland Raiders.

Antonio began the season slowly. He saw very little playing time in the first games of 2003. In one of those games, Antonio fumbled and lost the ball. His team lost. But that was not entirely Antonio's fault. With or without Antonio on the field, the Chargers were a bad team. They won only one of their first eight games and were on their way to the league's worst record.

As the team's playoff hopes disappeared, the coaches began giving more playing time to younger players, including their rookie tight end. In a game against the Minnesota Vikings on November 9, Antonio got his chance to shine. He only caught three passes during the game, but two were for big gains in yardage—25 and 26 yards—and one was a short toss for a touchdown. It was the best game of his new NFL career, and he helped the Chargers earn a rare victory.

A Strong Finish

As the coaches played him more, Antonio continued improving during the closing weeks of the 2003 season. He started the last nine games of the season. In four of those games, he had three or more catches. He even scored his second touchdown, and he did not fumble the ball again.

In spite of Antonio's best efforts, the Chargers ended the 2003 season with the terrible record of four wins and twelve losses. The Chargers defense allowed opponents to score too many times, and San Diego's offense depended too heavily on one player—LaDainian Tomlinson, their outstanding running back.

As he gained confidence, however, Antonio kept making his presence known. On December 14, in a match against the Green Bay Packers, Antonio put together an incredible game. In the Chargers' efforts to catch up to the Packers' score, Antonio made several big catches and plays. As in the game against the Vikings, Antonio made sure to fight for extra yards after catching the ball, and he gained 117 yards on his five receptions. His longest **catch-and-run** went for 48 yards—almost half the length of the field. Antonio's performance in this game was the first 100-yard receiving game by a Chargers rookie in almost 15 years. By the end of the 2003 season, Antonio, his team, his coaches, and the San Diego fans could not wait for the next season to begin.

ANTONIO GATES

Antonio plunges into the end zone to score his first career touchdown, November 9, 2003. The score came on a four-yard pass from Doug Flutie. Antonio's three catches for 55 yards helped the Chargers earn a 42 to 28 victory that day.

Looking Back, Looking Forward

Antonio liked San Diego, his team, and his fans, and he was prepared to devote himself to improving his level of play. Although his contract was only for two years, he knew that if he kept working hard his future would be assured. Teammate and superstar LaDainian Tomlinson said of Antonio's first season,

> "He was just feeling his way around pretty much all last year, then toward the end of the season we saw him kind of come into his own. Now, he has the potential to be one of the best."

Though the Chargers finished the 2003 season with a dismal record, Antonio gained national attention for his efforts. He finished with 24 receptions for 389 yards—an average of more than 16 yards per catch. Antonio had more receiving yardage than any other rookie tight end in 2003. Overall, Antonio finished fifth in total receiving yardage among all rookies—ahead of several players who had been chosen in the early rounds of the NFL draft.

By the end of the 2003 season Antonio's coaches and teammates had come to trust and respect his talent. However, Antonio knew that he still had a lot to learn. Although he had measured up well when compared to other rookies, Antonio knew his second season would provide a tougher test.

A New Jolt

Antonio's first game of the 2004 season, against the Houston Texans, set high expectations. Though he did not score a touchdown in the game, he surprised and dominated whoever tried to defend him, grabbing tough passes and either **eluding** or muscling past would-be tacklers for extra yards. Antonio made eight catches in the game against Houston, and he gained 123 yards. During the game, his single longest gain was 29 yards. Every one of his possessions improved the ability of his team to win the game.

The 2004 season marked a major turnaround for the Chargers. From winning just two of their first eight games in 2003, the Chargers won five of their first eight in 2004. Not only did they win frequently, but, in most of their games, they won big.

ANTONIO GATES

Their new starting tight end—a more comfortable and experienced Antonio Gates—made a noticeable contribution. Antonio started in every game in which he played during the 2004 season. His skills forced other teams to guard him closely. Because of the threat Antonio presented, defenders had to take attention away from the Chargers' other offensive weapon, LaDainian Tomlinson. In the first half of the season, the two Chargers stars combined to score 12 touchdowns.

Each game was a challenge to the Chargers to prove that their success was more than just a **fluke**. Other teams, coaches, and fans were still not convinced. Antonio kept honing his skills in order to meet the challenges each game brought.

Although he had natural skills with the ball, there was much more he needed to learn about playing the tight end position. In particular, he needed to improve his blocking. Antonio said about his new role in San Diego,

> **In high school, every last one of the passing schemes was designed for me. We either ran the ball or we threw it to me. But I was a terrible blocker in high school. All I wanted to do was catch the ball. The coaching staff here with the Chargers is showing me blocking techniques I'm really learning for the first time. I was never asked to block in high school so I was never in that situation and I wasn't interested.**

Antonio was interested now. He was interested in winning with what seemed to be a completely reenergized Chargers squad. The defense stepped up to complement the effort the offense was putting forth. The offense—driven by Antonio and Tomlinson—continued to produce touchdowns.

The Pro Bowl Case

A few minutes into the fourth quarter of their game against the Kansas City Chiefs on November 28, 2004, the Chargers were behind by a score of 23-17. After a long drive down the field, the Chargers

---

CROSS-CURRENTS

Read "The Playoffs and the Super Bowl" to learn more about how the NFL's postseason works. Go to page 50.

From Rookie to Pro Bowler 23

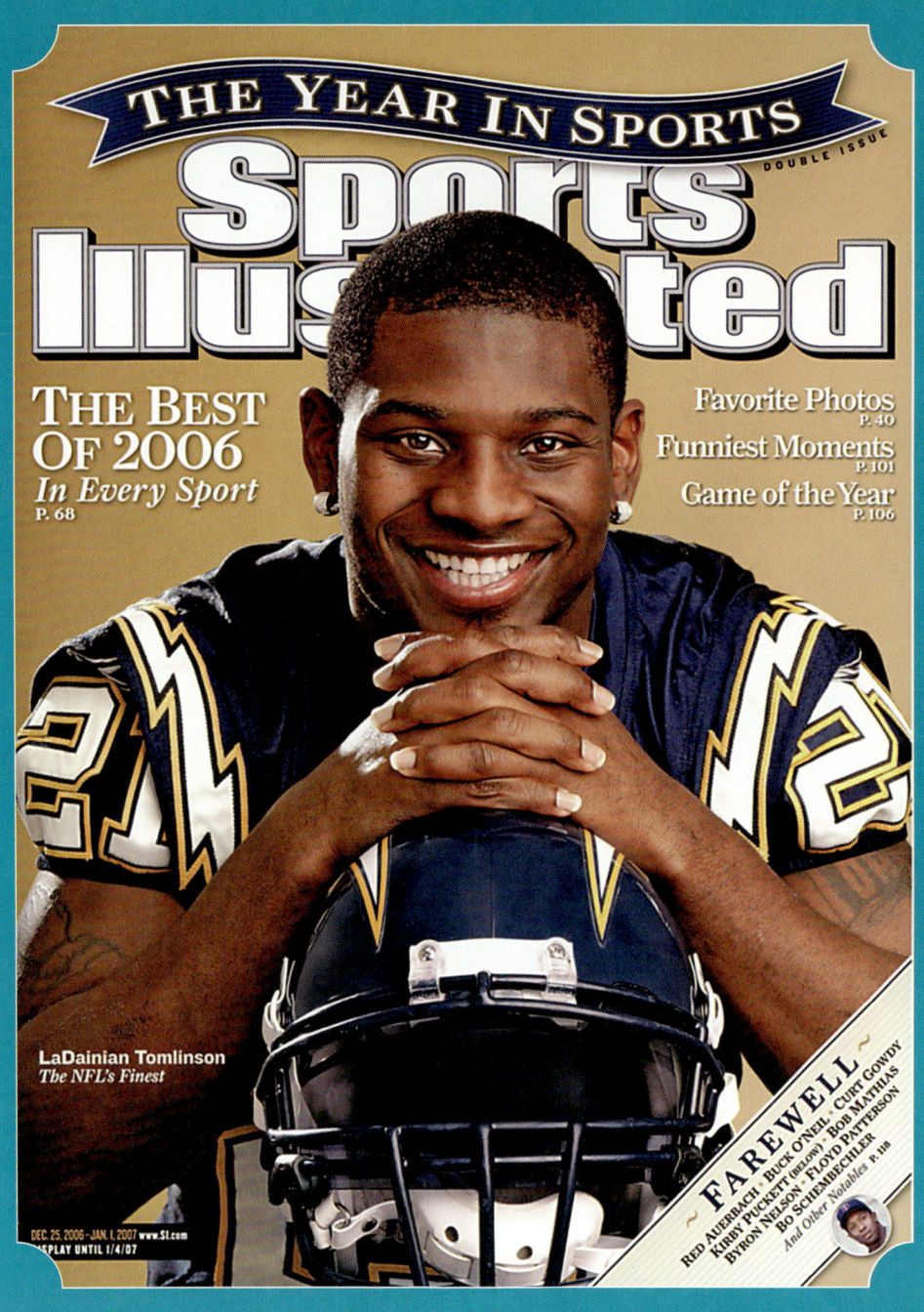

San Diego's LaDainian Tomlinson is pictured on a *Sports Illustrated* cover. Antonio's teammate was one of the league's best running backs. In 2004, Tomlinson led the NFL in rushing touchdowns scored, with 17.

ANTONIO GATES

Antonio breaks free for one of his two fourth-quarter touchdowns in the November 28, 2004, game against the Kansas City Chiefs. Antonio scored on passes of 18 and 11 yards to help San Diego earn a come-from-behind victory.

set up just inside the Chiefs' 20-yard line—the area known as the "red zone." The Chiefs tried to cover the Chargers' most likely targets, but Antonio broke free, snatching a pass and dashing into the end zone to tie the game at 23. The Chargers' **extra-point kick** gave them their first lead of the game. During the following kickoff, however, Chiefs kickoff returner Dante Hall ran the ball 96 yards for a touchdown. The Chiefs then completed a **two-point conversion** to take a seven-point lead.

The Chargers were stunned, but they put together another pass-heavy drive down the field and soon reached the Chiefs' red zone. The Chiefs were ready, but Antonio again slipped by their defense for an 11-yard touchdown. With the extra point, the game was tied at 31. Just over six minutes were left.

The Chiefs were unable to move the ball against the Chargers' defense, and San Diego's offense came back onto the field. The Chargers pushed down the field. With less than three minutes left, the Chargers kicked a **field goal** for the win. It was a huge game for Antonio—seven receptions for 92 yards and two touchdowns. More remarkable, it was the fourth game in a row in which he had scored. He had eight touchdowns in that four-game stretch.

The Chargers finished the 2004 season with a record of 12 wins and four losses—completely reversing their finish the season before. Plenty of praise fell on LaDainian Tomlinson, who had scored 17 touchdowns and run for more than 1,300 yards, and had caught 53 passes, including one for another touchdown. Almost as much of the spotlight, if not more, focused on Antonio Gates.

Antonio was suddenly the hottest young player in the NFL. In just his second season playing professional football, he earned his first Pro Bowl selection and his first All-Pro selection. Also, by scoring 13 touchdowns Antonio set the single-season all-time record for a tight end. Previously, four players had shared the record of 12 touchdowns by a tight end: Mike Ditka (1961), Jerry Smith (1967), Todd Christensen (1983), and Wesley Walls (1999).

San Diego's winning season ended with an overtime loss to the New York Jets in the first game of the playoffs. The defeat was disappointing, but it helped show the Chargers where they needed to improve, and it gave them something to aim for in the seasons to come: playoff victories.

CROSS-CURRENTS
To learn what it means for a player to be selected for the All-Pro Team, read "All-Pro Status." Go to page 51.

4
BIG MONEY, BIG GAMES

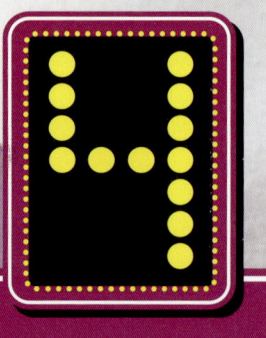

In spite of their early exit from the 2004 playoffs, the success of Antonio Gates and his teammates during the regular season created energy and confidence on the San Diego Chargers that the team had not felt in years. It was the first season since 1995 that the Chargers had won more than half of their games.

Before beginning his off-season training, Antonio played in his first Pro Bowl. Antonio caught just three passes, but he gained 33 yards on one of them and scored a touchdown on another, helping the AFC team to victory. The Pro Bowl allowed Antonio to end his second NFL season on a high note.

Big Money, Big Games   27

Antonio hauls in a pass during an October 2005 game against the Oakland Raiders. The star tight end was happy with the contract that he signed with San Diego after his All-Pro performance during 2004.

A Big Contract

Antonio's first contract expired at the end of his second season. Much of Antonio's attention in the off-season—and the attention of his team and fans—centered on negotiations over renewing his contract.

Antonio knew San Diego was a good place for him, but he also wanted the Chargers' owners to recognize that his Pro Bowl status greatly increased his value. Antonio's agent, Andre Colona, was famous for getting as much money as he could out of team owners. The owners of the Chargers appreciated Antonio and wanted to keep him on the team, but they were afraid of paying too much for a

CROSS-CURRENTS
If you'd like to find out more about the contracts and salaries of NFL players, read "Money Matters." Go to page 52.

ANTONIO GATES

player who had only been in the league for two years. As the deadline for signing his contract passed, Antonio held out and did not report to training camp on time. When he did show up and sign the contract a few days later, Antonio blamed the delay on travel difficulties. Once the contract was signed, Antonio was happy, and he said,

> "I think I got Antonio Gates money. I think that was fair enough for me, and it's a good situation for me to be here long term."

Antonio's new contract did not make him the highest-paid tight end in the league, but it put him close to the top. It is believed that Antonio made between $10 and $11 million over the first two years of the six-year deal.

Back on the Gridiron

The Chargers' first game of 2005 was against the Dallas Cowboys. According to team rules, Antonio could not play because he was late to training camp. The Chargers had fewer offensive options without him. The Cowboys intercepted passes by Chargers quarterback Drew Brees twice and **hampered** Tomlinson's running game enough to win the game.

Even though they lost, the Chargers looked forward to the rest of the season. The team and its fans were glad Antonio was back in the lineup. Antonio knew he had to prove to his team and fans that he was worth the money. After signing his new contract, Antonio knew he would have to continue working hard:

> "The biggest key for a successful player is avoiding complacency. You see a lot of guys get the money and fame, then become complacent with where they are. I promised myself I would never let that happen. No matter who you are or where you are, you can always get better."

A Trio of Touchdowns

When the Chargers faced off against Kansas City in San Diego on October 30, they had only three wins in six games. Their fans were ready to see some sparks.

Big Money, Big Games 29

Linebacker Derrick Johnson tries to stop Antonio during the Chiefs-Chargers game on October 30, 2005. In one of his best games of the season, Antonio caught 10 passes for 145 yards and three touchdowns as the Chargers won, 28-20.

ANTONIO GATES

Late in the first quarter, with the score tied at zero, the Chargers pushed into the Chiefs red zone. Antonio positioned himself close to the sideline. A Chiefs safety lined up across from him, but Antonio calmly watched his quarterback for the signal. After the snap, Antonio faked with his hips and shoulders, fooling his defender and leaving him behind. Antonio then easily caught a pass from quarterback Drew Brees and raced into the end zone to give his team the lead. He was just getting started.

In the last seconds of the first half, Brees lofted a pass into the end zone from just behind the Chiefs' 20-yard line. As the ball dropped downward, it looked like the pass was going to be intercepted. Then Antonio leaped into the air, soaring above two Chiefs. He grabbed the pass and hit the ground for his second touchdown of the game. The Chargers trotted off the field at halftime to the roar of the crowd.

The Chiefs came back strong in the second half, scoring two touchdowns without response from the Chargers and moving within a single score of taking the lead. With about ten minutes left in the game, Antonio lined up in the traditional tight end spot, close to the linemen. The ball snapped, and Antonio ran a short route across the middle of the field. Brees tossed him a quick pass, and a defender was on him almost as soon as he caught it. Antonio shifted his weight, put on a burst of speed, and broke away. Other defenders closed in as well, so Antonio tucked the ball to his chest and the race was on. Antonio's long strides ate up the yards, and he bolted into the end zone for a third touchdown. The fans went wild.

Top Tight End

Even with strong performances and wins like the one on October 30, the Chargers managed to win just nine of the 2005 season's 16 games—not enough to make the playoffs. Five of their seven defeats, however, were by fewer than five points. The Chargers again set about improving themselves in the off-season.

Antonio still had one game left. He had again been selected to take part in the Pro Bowl. He only caught two passes in the game, but that was not unusual given all the superstars on the field. The catches that had brought him to the Pro Bowl were the important ones.

Although he sprained his ankle about two-thirds of the way through the 2005 season, Antonio still set personal and league records

Big Money, Big Games

for receiving. He caught 89 passes and he gained 1,101 yards. By scoring 10 touchdowns, he led all tight ends in the league for the second straight season. Antonio also became one of two tight ends in NFL history to record 1,100 receiving yards and ten touchdowns in a single season. The other was Todd Christensen, who had 1,200 yards and 12 touchdowns with the Oakland Raiders in 1983.

Antonio's remarkable offensive numbers brought on talk about how far he could go. Earlier in his career, he responded to such talk by saying,

CROSS-CURRENTS

For more on how Antonio has helped redefine the skills needed for his position, read "The New Tight Ends." Go to page 52.

Antonio (right) speaks with reporters about being selected for the 2006 Pro Bowl. With him are (from left) former Detroit running back Barry Sanders, New York Giants defensive end Michael Strahan, and Kansas City Chiefs tight end Tony Gonzalez.

ANTONIO GATES

Both teammates and opponents praise Antonio's ability. "The new-age tight end is way more athletic and physical, and he can really stretch the field," said Steelers linebacker James Farrior. "That's what Antonio Gates does. He's not a normal tight end."

Big Money, Big Games

> **"I believe potential is a dangerous word; it can be used for anybody. . . . I don't want people to always say, 'He has the potential to be good.' Or, 'He has a couple of years to go.' I want somebody to say, ' . . . [T]hat's a good tight end.' Period."**

Life in the Big Leagues

One hard part of life as a pro athlete is the intense media attention that comes with fame. Since entering the NFL, Antonio has not shared many personal details about himself. He is single, although he did mention that he has a daughter in a 2004 interview.

Another tough part of pro-sports life is the trades and free-agent signings that break up team partnerships. Early in 2006, quarterback Drew Brees left the Chargers to join the New Orleans Saints. Philip Rivers, a 2004 draftee and former college star, stepped into the role of starting quarterback for the Chargers. Rivers had only played four games in his first two seasons, but the Chargers had high expectations. The Chargers also picked up linebacker Shawne Merriman, an outstanding defender. Armed with the skill and energy of their younger players, San Diego was again ready for the season to begin.

Scoring When It Counts

Antonio started every game in the 2006 season, and he cemented his reputation for making big plays when it mattered most. At the start of their 13th game of the season, the Chargers had an excellent record of ten wins and two losses, and they were about to clinch a playoff spot. Their opponent was the Denver Broncos, a strong team, but the Chargers were on a six-game winning streak and not about to stop. Antonio caught two touchdown passes in the game, and Tomlinson ran for three touchdowns. The Chargers crushed the Broncos, and Antonio's **stat line**—seven catches for 104 yards—showed the big role he played in the victory.

Antonio was not only catching, running, and scoring at a high level, but his blocking and understanding of the game had also improved. Older players, like tight end Brandon Manumaleuna, appreciated Antonio's work ethic and team play. The veterans gave

ANTONIO GATES

Antonio stretches for the ball, fighting off pressure from New England's James Sanders and Chad Scott, during the NFL playoffs, January 14, 2007. Despite Antonio's six catches for 61 yards, the Patriots defeated the Chargers, 24-21.

him tips on how to improve his play when he did not have the ball. Antonio became confident that he could help his team win in many ways:

> **"I always anticipate going out and playing well. And that doesn't always mean me catching passes. At any given time, it could be any other player that catches the ball. It's doing whatever it takes to help this team come away with a victory."**

Antonio scored a touchdown in the last game of the season, bringing his 2006 total to nine, and the Chargers ended the season on a 10-game winning streak. Antonio's efforts made a big contribution to their 14-2 record. The amazing contribution of LaDainian Tomlinson was also a huge factor. With 31 touchdowns, Tomlinson set the all-time league record for a single season.

The Chargers went into the playoffs with high hopes. Their first game was against the powerful New England Patriots. Although the Chargers led for most of the game, the Patriots came from behind in the fourth quarter and won by a field goal, 24-21.

The Chargers were disappointed about the way their season had ended. For Antonio and his teammates, playoff success and a Super Bowl victory was the ultimate goal.

CHARGING AHEAD

After leading his team in all receiving categories in the 2006 season and being selected for his third consecutive Pro Bowl and All-Pro teams, Antonio Gates looked ahead to improving both his individual and his team skills. It was clear that only a major team effort would bring the Chargers the glory they felt they deserved.

The Art of Building a Team

Antonio also began working to build a stronger bond with quarterback Philip Rivers. They were close in age. Antonio and Rivers started to train and exercise together, practice passing routes and patterns, and hang out at Rivers's house. Rivers said of Antonio's improvement and their chemistry,

Charging Ahead

Because of his size, speed, and ability to catch passes, many football experts consider Antonio the best tight end in the NFL. He had another fine season in 2007, catching 75 passes for 984 yards and nine touchdowns.

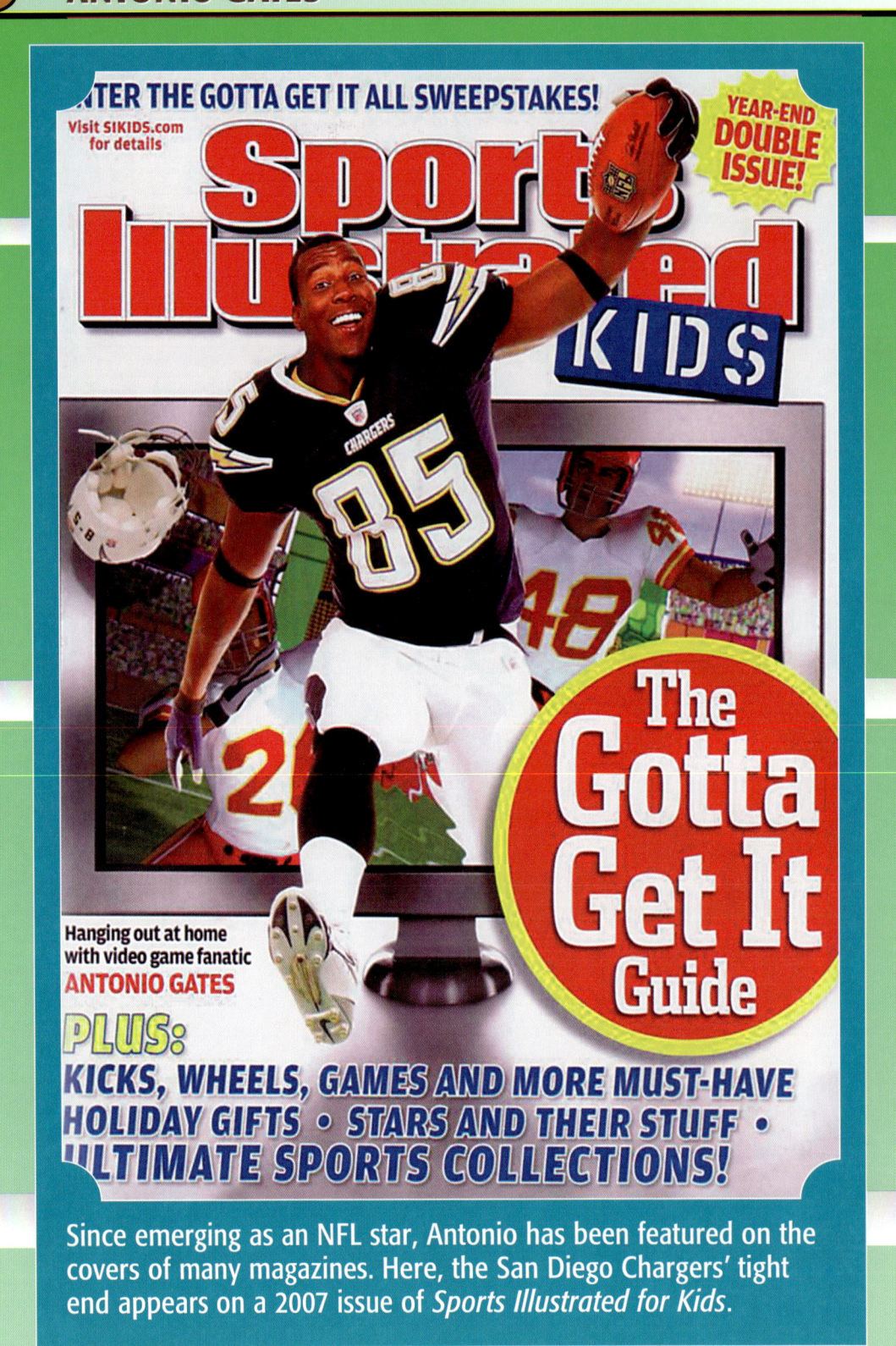

ANTONIO GATES

Since emerging as an NFL star, Antonio has been featured on the covers of many magazines. Here, the San Diego Chargers' tight end appears on a 2007 issue of *Sports Illustrated for Kids*.

Charging Ahead

> **"He's more patient when he runs routes. You can see he trusts the plays more because he's not trying to force anything. Plus, he knows that even when he's double-covered, he's still open in my mind."**

To a player as skilled as Antonio, double coverage—or being guarded by two defenders at one time—is a fact of life. When the defense focuses on Antonio, however, chances open up for other players like Rivers and Tomlinson to make big plays.

For some time, Antonio has drawn attention not just on the field but off of it as well. Sportswriters took great pleasure and used up lots of space in newspapers and magazines discussing the Chargers' number 85. They even compared up-and-coming tight ends to him. Antonio responded to these comparisons by saying,

> **"It's one of those things where you hear it and you get a pat on the back, but at the same time you understand that you're only as good as you performed in your last game. I still work hard because every year a new tight end comes out and it's a challenge to me when somebody says something like 'This guy is the next Antonio Gates.' I'm the guy saying there isn't going to be another Antonio Gates, so that's the challenge that I hold, and I hold myself accountable to making myself better as a player."**

The Gift of Fame

In addition to helping set high expectations for the Chargers, Antonio also became an icon for young people around the world. He starred in the *Madden NFL* football video game series and was featured on the cover of *Sports Illustrated for Kids*. As he became famous, Antonio took the opportunity to promote kids' health and help children in need.

In the summer of 2004, Antonio took part in and sponsored "Shoot to Cure HD," a free throw-shooting event in which he used his basketball skills to help raise money for the **Huntington's**

CROSS-CURRENTS

If you'd like to learn more about the history of San Diego's NFL franchise, check out "Charger Mania." Go to page 54.

Disease Society of America. Antonio is also a leading spokesperson for NFL Play 60, an organization run by the NFL that works to fight childhood **obesity**. Founded in 2007, Play 60 representatives visit schools and run camps where they encourage kids to do 60 minutes of exercise a day. When working with children, Antonio talks about the importance of regular exercise, eating healthy, not eating too much, stretching, and warming up before playing sports. While talking about Thanksgiving with an interviewer for *NFLRush*, Antonio said,

> "You pay the price for eating so much, you know. I try to jog and do some cardio after eating a lot."

Also in 2007, Antonio participated in the NFL's "Take a Player to School" program. He accompanied a boy named Kody to his class in Escondido, California. In addition, Antonio regularly takes part in an annual blood drive around Thanksgiving to raise money and awareness for children living in poverty.

The 2007 Surge

When the football season began again, Antonio gathered his energies and returned his focus to his team and the football field. For Antonio and the Chargers, the first game of the 2007 season was against the Chicago Bears, the team that had lost the Super Bowl the year before. At halftime, the Bears led the game by three points. Less than a minute into the third quarter, however, Antonio snagged a pass from Tomlinson (who occasionally acts as quarterback on trick plays) and sprinted into the end zone for the Chargers' first touchdown and the lead. The Chargers beat the Bears 14-3, filling their home crowd with high hopes for the season. The team's next three games, however, were losses.

In their fifth game, against a tough Denver Broncos defense, Antonio had one of his best games. During the Chargers' first offensive drive of the game, Antonio lined up on the outside. Champ Bailey, a seven-time Pro Bowler and three-time All-Pro **cornerback**, lined up against him. At the snap, Antonio moved like he was running toward the center of the field but then dashed toward the sideline. He got away from Bailey, caught a pass from Rivers, and

Charging Ahead

Antonio bowls over two Chicago defenders after catching a pass during the Chargers' game against the Bears, September 9, 2007. Antonio caught nine passes for 107 yards and a touchdown as San Diego won, 14-3.

ran for 23 yards before Denver defenders could stop him. Rivers said of that play,

> **I haven't seen anyone do that [to] Champ in any film I've watched.**

Antonio gained 113 yards and a touchdown on seven catches, helping the Chargers end their losing streak and start a streak of wins.

A little more than halfway through the season, the Chargers' record was 5-5, and their playoff hopes were on the line. Their eleventh game took place in San Diego against a strong Baltimore Ravens team. The first quarter was scoreless, but in the second quarter a scoring rampage began. The Chargers scored a field goal, but the Ravens struck back with a touchdown. Antonio then turned the game around for the Chargers. Rushing past defenders, he caught a pass from Rivers and ran 35 yards for a touchdown. Before halftime, the Chargers took over the game, scoring another touchdown and two more field goals.

At the start of the third quarter, Antonio again got through the Ravens' defense and caught a pass from Rivers for a 25-yard touchdown. His touchdown put the Chargers so far ahead the Ravens could not catch them. Antonio finished the game with six catches for 105 yards and two touchdowns. The Chargers went on to win their next five games and end the season with an 11-5 record.

Dreams and Pain: the Postseason

Antonio finished the 2007 regular season with nine touchdowns and 984 yards, the second-most yardage in his career. He was selected for his fourth Pro Bowl.

Although the Chargers entered the playoffs as an underdog, the squad was full of energy and momentum from their season-ending streak of wins. San Diego's first game was against the Tennessee Titans. The Chargers won the game, but Antonio dislocated his left big toe while playing. The injury sounds small, but it hampered his ability to make quick moves and accelerate while running.

In the next playoff game, the Chargers played the Indianapolis Colts—the defending Super Bowl champions. It was a close, tough game, but the Chargers eventually won, 28-24, with the help of strong defensive plays. During the game, Antonio's injured toe got worse. He finished with just two catches for 28 yards. In addition, both Rivers and Tomlinson left the game early because of injuries.

In the AFC Championship game—the last game before the Super Bowl—the Chargers faced the New England Patriots. The Patriots had gone undefeated for the entire 2007 season and were widely regarded as one of the best teams in NFL history. Although Antonio, Tomlinson, and Rivers were seriously injured, the three players all started the game. Tomlinson had to leave the game after just a few plays, but Antonio hung in there. However, he managed just two

Charging Ahead

catches for 17 yards. With San Diego's stars unable to play effectively, the Chargers could manage just four field goals in a 21-12 loss.

A few days after their playoff defeat, the Chargers revealed that both Antonio and Rivers needed surgery. Both players would need long periods of rest to recover from their injuries.

Bolts on the Horizon

Looking forward to the 2008 season, the Chargers hoped their much-improved defense would be complemented by a strong, healthy offense. If the Chargers' wide receiver, running back, quarterback, and tight end were all healthy, they would challenge opposing defenses and open up opportunities for big plays and big scores.

With Antonio slowed by a foot injury, San Diego struggled to score touchdowns against the unbeaten New England Patriots in the AFC Championship game. The Chargers managed just four field goals in the disappointing 21-12 loss.

ANTONIO GATES

Antonio worked hard to recover from his foot injury. He told reporters that his goal for 2008 was to "be the [number] 85 that people are used to me being in the past. I think that's part of the challenge."

Since the beginning of the 2004 season, only two players in the league have caught more touchdown passes than Antonio Gates. These two are Marvin Harrison and Randy Moss. Harrison and Moss are arguably two of the best receivers to ever play the game.

Antonio had surgery for his toe injury at the end of February 2008. The amount of time needed to recover is hard to predict because of the large number of muscles, tendons, and ligaments involved in the operation. His team and fans were worried about the future of their superstar tight end, but in response to their concerns Antonio said,

> "It's crazy how far I've come in this short period of time. It's just determining when I'm going to be ready. I know I'm going to be ready. It's just when."

Five seasons into his professional football career, Antonio's catching and running have been consistently impressive. While his toe injury certainly slowed him down at the end of the 2007 season, he still made tough catches and did what he could to help his team. Equally impressive, Antonio has fumbled the ball only once in his whole professional career—an astounding statistic considering how often the ball is in his hands.

Antonio Gates is still young. He should have several more seasons to show off his touchdown-catching talents for Chargers fans. By the time Antonio's career ends, he may well make good on the wish he expressed in a 2006 interview:

> "You never hear people say they come to the game to watch the tight end, . . . but I want to be that guy. I want to be known as the most exciting tight end to ever play this game."

CROSS-CURRENTS

For some information about past players that Antonio has been compared to, read "The Great Tight Ends." Go to page 55.

A Tight End's Universe

A tight end, known as a "TE," is part of a football team's offensive line. Also on the offensive line are the center, the guards, and the tackles. The two guards line up on either side of the center. The two tackles line up on either side of the guards. Depending on the play, the tight end usually lines up alongside either the right or left tackle. The quarterback stands just behind the center in order to catch the ball when the center snaps it. Behind the quarterback are the running backs.

Tight ends have a tough job. They have two offensive roles, both of which require them to be bruisers. The traditional job of the tight end is to catch short passes in the middle of the field and then take the hard tackle from the other team's defensive backs. Tight ends also work as an additional blocker to protect running backs and the quarterback.

Defending against a tight end's offensive moves are the other team's linebackers or cornerbacks. Although cornerbacks are usually fast and agile, their relatively small size often makes it hard for them to tackle a tight end. Linebackers are larger and stronger, but if they are defending against a pass to a tight end, it takes them away from their main duty, which is to stop an offense's running game. (Go back to page 6.)

The Pro Bowl Story

The Pro Bowl is an all-star game for the NFL. Only the very best players at each position are chosen to attend. Players are selected for the two 43-man teams by a voting process. One-third of the decision-making power lies in each of three groups—fans, coaches, and NFL players—and their ballots are averaged to determine which players will take part in the game.

The two teams in the game are divided along conference lines. For organizational and historical reasons, the NFL is split into the American Football Conference (AFC) and the National Football Conference (NFC). The first Pro Bowl as we know it today took place on January 24, 1971, in Los Angeles. The NFC beat the AFC by a score of 27 to 6. Famed Oakland Raiders coach and present-day football analyst John Madden coached the AFC team, while San Francisco 49ers coach Dick Nolan coached the NFC. In 1980, the Pro Bowl was played at Aloha Stadium in Honolulu, Hawaii, and the game has been played there ever since.

The Pro Bowl game is always scheduled for early February, usually a weekend or two after the Super Bowl, which is the NFL championship game. After the Super Bowl decides the best team in the league, the Pro Bowl showcases the league's best players. Although the event is

◀◀ CROSS-CURRENTS ▶▶   47

The Pro Bowl is held at Aloha stadium in Honolulu, Hawaii, each year. The game is played a week after the Super Bowl. Antonio has been selected to the AFC's Pro Bowl squad four times.

mostly just for show, being chosen to take part in the Pro Bowl game increases players' fame, their value to their teams, and the respect they receive on and off the field.

Only a few players make the Pro Bowl many times. Given how hard football is on players' bodies, staying at the top of the game for numerous years is far more difficult than just staying in the league—which is hard enough. Some players, however, have been able to stay on top for many years. Junior Seau, who played for New England in 2007, was selected to the Pro Bowl 12 times—all with the Chargers. The record holders for the most Pro Bowl selections are Merlin Olsen, a defensive lineman who played from 1962 to 1976, and Bruce Matthews, an offensive lineman who played from 1983 to 2000, with 14 each. Tony Gonzalez, a record-setting tight end with Kansas City, has been selected for nine Pro Bowls.

(Go back to page 8.) ◀◀

NCAA March Madness

March Madness is the nickname for the tournament that decides which team is the champion of NCAA Division I college basketball. The tournament has six rounds and starts with 64 teams. Each round cuts that number in half. After the first two rounds, the Sweet Sixteen, the Elite Eight, and the Final Four lead up to the championship game.

At the beginning of March Madness, each team is seeded. This involves ranking teams from first to 16th in one of four tournament brackets. A committee of sportswriters, coaches, and NCAA officials decides where each team should be seeded in the tournament. A team's regular season record and performance is taken heavily into account. The March Madness tournament is organized so that the lowest-seeded teams play the highest-seeded teams in the first round. The idea is to set up the tournament so that the best teams play against each other at the end—if lower-seeded teams do not beat them.

Even though Antonio didn't participate in March Madness until his junior year of college, he made the most of his time in the tournament. The Kent State Golden Flashes entered the 2002 tournament seeded 10th in their bracket. Antonio and the Golden Flashes beat Oklahoma State, which was seeded seventh, in the first round of the NCAA tournament. Kent State next faced the second-seeded University of Alabama, which was the Southeastern Conference (SEC) champion and a championship contender. The Golden Flashes ran away with the game, winning 71-58, and the nation watched as they entered their next game against the University of Pittsburgh, the number three seed. With 43 seconds left in the game, Antonio made two free throws to give his team a three-point lead, and Pitt could not make the shots to catch up. The Golden Flashes won, 78-73, with 22 points scored by Antonio.

The Golden Flashes' next game was against fifth-seeded Indiana University. Indiana controlled the game by making 15 three-point shots. Antonio again scored 22 points and played very well, helping bring his team within seven points during the fourth quarter, but Kent State could not withstand Indiana's offense and lost, 81-69. Indiana eventually came in second place in the entire tournament.

(Go back to page 14.)

Undrafted and Free

In sports, a free agent is a player who is not bound to a team by any form of signed contract. That player is free to play for any team he or she chooses, assuming the team wants the player to join them.

In the NFL, an undrafted free agent is a player who was not selected in the NFL draft but still wants to play in the league. Teams can sign undrafted free agents for the league minimum salary, which as of 2007 was $285,000 a year. Drafted players have the right to negotiate for more money. The low cost of signing undrafted free agents encourages teams to take chances on and explore—and sometimes exploit—the talent and energy of young players. Such players do not have much to bargain with since they are new to the league and have not yet built up experience or a reputation. If successful, undrafted players offer incredible value. In the case of Antonio Gates, the San Diego Chargers probably had not made a better investment in over ten years. Other successful NFL players who began as unsigned free agents include Kurt Warner, Wes Welker, Rod Smith, Willie Parker, Priest Holmes, Jake Delhomme, and Wayne Chrebet.

(Go back to page 14.)

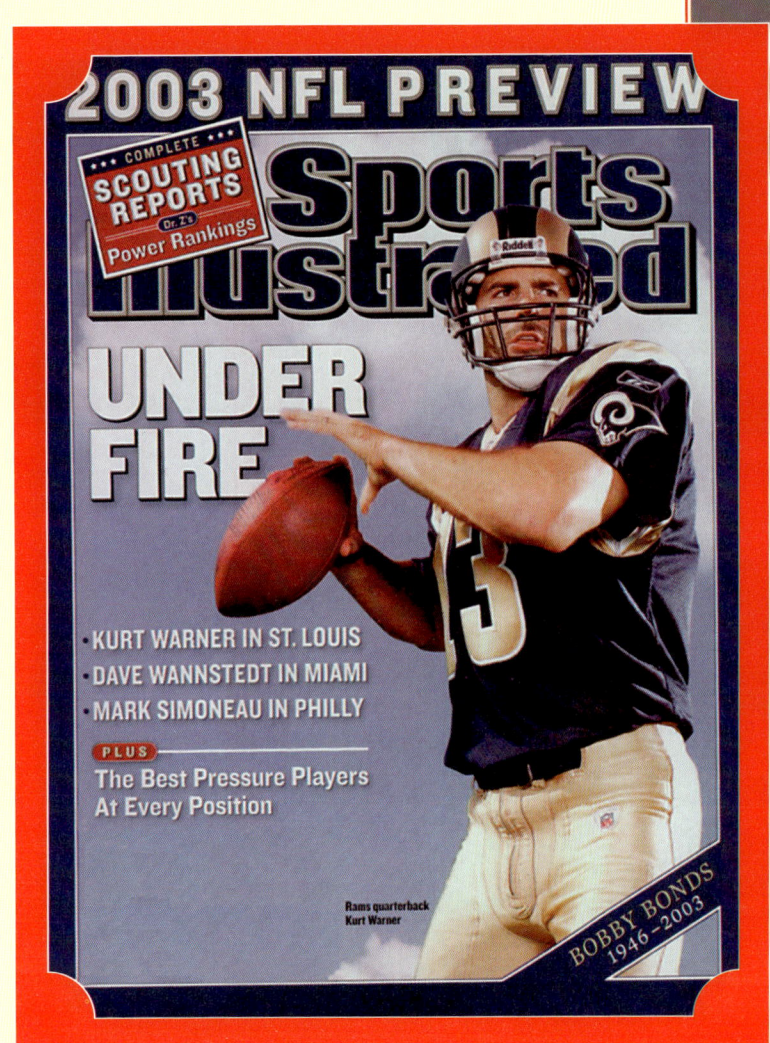

Kurt Warner, pictured here on the cover of Sports Illustrated in 2003, was never drafted into the NFL. The quarterback played several seasons in the Arena Football League before getting a chance to play with the NFL's St. Louis Rams.

CROSS-CURRENTS

The Playoffs and the Super Bowl

The NFL regular season occupies the attention of millions of people for almost half of every year. The drama of the regular season leads up to the playoffs and the Super Bowl—major games in which the smallest mistake and the biggest play go down in NFL history.

The NFL is divided into two conferences—the American Football Conference and the National Football Conference. The AFC and the NFC each has its own playoff tournament to determine the conference champions. The two conference champions play in the Super Bowl—the championship game of the whole NFL.

Each conference has four divisions. The teams with the best records in their divisions at the end of the regular season are the division champions. The division champions proceed to the playoffs, in which they are seeded first through fourth according to their finishing records. Apart from the division champions, the two next best teams from each conference also join the playoffs as "wild cards." The wild cards are seeded fifth and sixth. In the NFL playoffs, each round is single-elimination. The stakes are high. Either a team wins and makes it to the next round or loses and is out completely.

In the first round of the playoffs for each conference, the third-seeded team

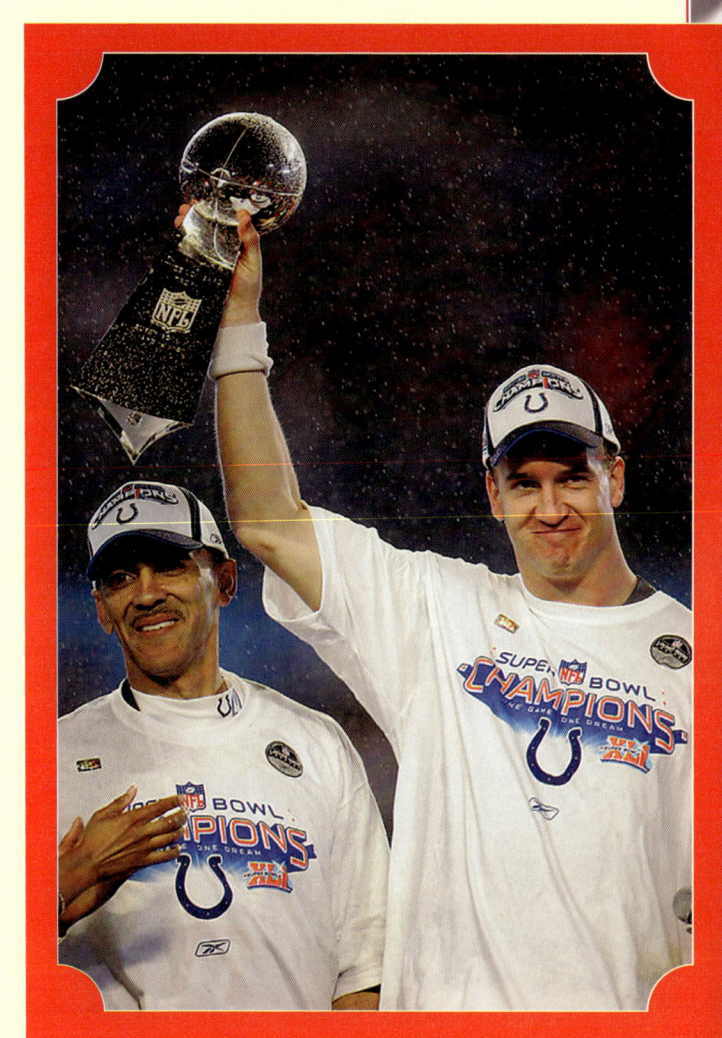

Indianapolis coach Tony Dungy (left) smiles as Peyton Manning lifts the Lombardi Trophy to celebrate the Colts' victory in Super Bowl XLI. All NFL teams begin their seasons hoping to win the Super Bowl.

plays the sixth-seeded team, and the fourth-seeded team plays the fifth-seeded team. The winners of these games go to the second round. The first- and second-seeded teams get a free ride to the second round of the playoffs, in which they play the winners from the first round. After the second round comes the conference finals, in which the second-round winners play each other. The winners of each conference's finals meet in the Super Bowl. As the most important game of the NFL season—and the biggest game an NFL player can hope to play in—the Super Bowl is usually charged with emotion. The winner of the Super Bowl receives the Vince Lombardi Trophy, which is named after the legendary Green Bay Packers coach who died just before the 1970 season.

The first professional football championship game that is now called the Super Bowl was held in 1967 between the Green Bay Packers, champions of the National Football League, and the Kansas City Chiefs, champions of the American Football League. The first NFL Super Bowl took place in 1971 following the merger of the two leagues into the NFL.

(Go back to page 22.)

All-Pro Status

"All-Pro" is short for the **Associated Press** NFL All-Pro Team. Begun in the 1940s, the All-Pro is football's oldest selection awards program. Each year, a committee of Associated Press members votes for the NFL's best players at each position. In addition to the "All-Pro" label, they give players "first-team" and "second-team" status. The players who get the most votes are the first-team All-Pros; the runners-up are the second-team All-Pros. All-Pro players do not play in a special game, but like being chosen to play in the Pro Bowl, being voted All-Pro is a sign of a season of outstanding achievement.

Some players have made the All-Pro team many times. The 2007 All-Pro Team features several of these All-Pro veterans. On the offense, running back LaDainian Tomlinson has earned six selections, second-team quarterback Brett Favre has earned seven, receiver Randy Moss has earned four, receiver Terrell Owens has earned five, tackle Walter Jones has earned seven, guard Alan Faneca has earned five, and center Jeff Saturday has earned three. On the defense, cornerback Champ Bailey has earned four All-Pro selections, tackle Kevin Williams has earned three, and safety Ed Reed has earned four. Jerry Rice, one of the most decorated and successful players in NFL history, made the All-Pro team 12 times. Rice retired in 2005.

(Go back to page 25.)

Money Matters

Money matters in professional football. With rising ticket prices, corporate-sponsored stadiums, massive salaries for star players, and huge endorsement contracts, money plays a big role in the decisions of players, coaches, and even teams when they decide where to play.

NFL teams are operated like large corporations. They deal with millions of dollars every year. In addition to players and coaches, NFL teams require huge staffs, from scouts to assistant trainers to media specialists. NFL teams are constantly making deals with other teams and negotiating contracts with players and their agents. Agents compete with each other for the right to represent players. They are responsible for negotiating contracts for the players. In return for getting good contracts for their players, agents receive a percentage of the profits.

The NFL Players Association is a group that provides many services to NFL players. The Players Association negotiates the basic terms for the relationships between teams, players, and the league. It also provides financial advisors to help athletes manage their wealth and presents opportunities for players to get involved in charities. (Go back to page 27.)

The New Tight Ends

Antonio Gates is a leading member of a relatively new group of talented tight ends who are more adept at catching the ball and gaining yardage. These new tight ends are changing the way that football is played in the NFL. Coaches and teams still want their tight ends to block and provide protection for their running backs and quarterbacks. However, NFL coaches also want their tight ends to run creative short and long routes and catch the ball.

A large tight end who can make big catches and run after the catch is a great weapon for a football team. Like Antonio Gates, many of the NFL's other top tight ends today are very good at scoring touchdowns.

Tony Gonzalez was the first of this new generation of tight ends. He is still one of the best at his position in the league. Gonzalez joined the Kansas City Chiefs in 1997. Since then, he has caught 820 passes and scored 66 touchdowns—both records for NFL tight ends. Tony has over 10,000 receiving yards in his career. He has been selected for the Pro Bowl nine times, and has been named an All-Pro four times.

◀◀ CROSS-CURRENTS ▶▶

Jason Witten was drafted by the Dallas Cowboys in 2003. Since then, he has been selected to four Pro Bowls. In the 2007 season, Witten set career bests for catches (96), receiving yardage (1,145), and touchdowns (seven). As a result, he was named to the All-Pro team for the first time.

Dallas Clark, tight end for the Indianapolis Colts, caught 58 passes for 616 yards, and set a team record for a tight end with 11 touchdown catches in 2007. In the first five years of his career, Clark has caught 179 passes, including 25 touchdowns.

Kellen Winslow Jr. is the son of Hall of Fame tight end Kellen Winslow Sr. His career has been slowed because of injuries, but in 2006 he led all tight ends in catches, with 89. The next season, he had 82 receptions for 1,106 yards and was selected for the AFC's Pro Bowl team for the first time.

Alge Crumpler has played tight end for the Atlanta Falcons since 2001. He has 316 career catches, including 35 touchdowns. Crumpler has gone to four Pro Bowls and was named to the All-Pro team in 2003 and 2006.

(Go back to page 31.) ◀◀

Tony Gonzalez of the Kansas City Chiefs celebrates after catching his 63rd career touchdown pass, October 14, 2007. That catch set a new record for most touchdowns scored by a tight end.

54 ◀◀ CROSS-CURRENTS ▶▶

Charger Mania

The Chargers originated in the American Football League as the Los Angeles Chargers in 1960, but the team moved to San Diego in 1961. They had a few good years right after the move, but they slumped between 1966 and 1979. The San Diego Chargers then reached the playoffs for four straight years, but they never made it past the AFC Conference Finals.

The team struggled again for another ten years. In 1995, the Chargers made it to Super Bowl XXIX to face the San Francisco 49ers. No one expected the Chargers to get as far in the playoffs as they did. The 49ers, behind quarterback Steve Young and receiver Jerry Rice—both of whom would later enter the Pro Football Hall of Fame—were determined not to be upset in the year's biggest game. The 49ers beat the Chargers, 49-26. In the game, Steve Young made history by throwing six touchdown passes, setting a Super Bowl record that still stands. Jerry Rice caught three of those passes.

The Chargers did not again win a playoff game until the current era of Antonio and LaDainian Tomlinson. Their 2006 record of 14 wins and 2 losses was the best in the team's history and gave Chargers fans hope for the future success of their team.

(Go back to page 39.) ◀◀

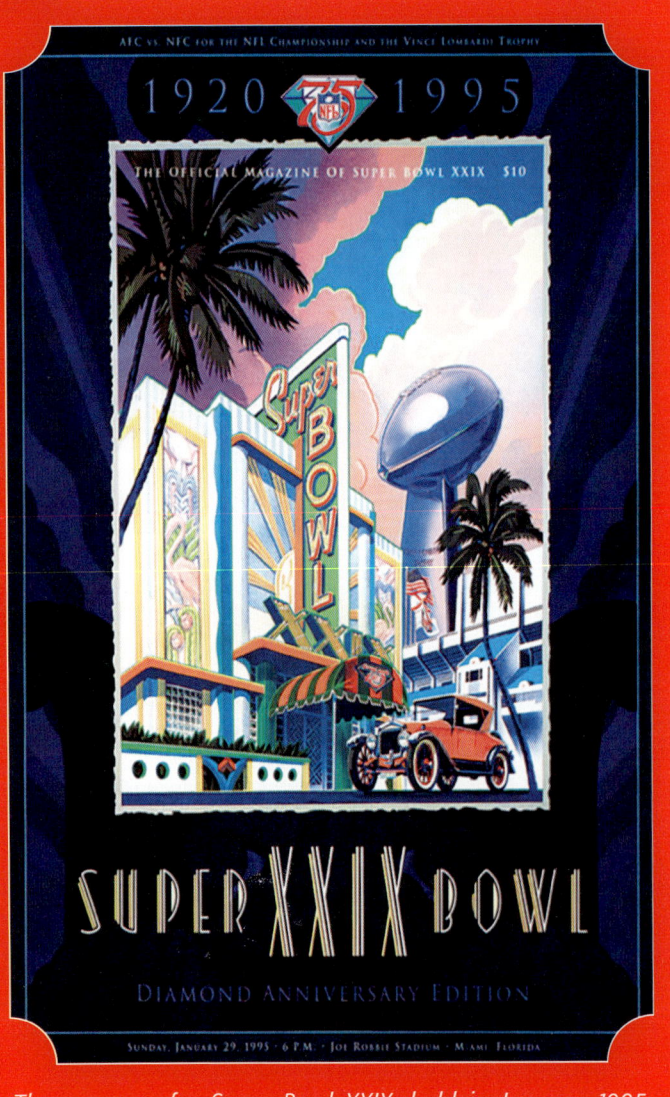

The program for Super Bowl XXIX, held in January 1995 between the Chargers and the San Francisco 49ers. San Francisco jumped out to a quick lead, and easily defeated the Chargers, 49-26.

The Great Tight Ends

As Antonio Gates gathered more glory, people began comparing him to great players of his position from the past. Among the top tight in NFL history are Kellen Winslow Sr., Mike Ditka, and John Mackey.

Kellen Winslow, Sr., who played tight end for the San Diego Chargers from 1979 to 1987, was a skilled blocker and an excellent receiver. Over the course of his career, Winslow scored 45 touchdowns. He was also a three-time All-Pro, and he went to the Pro Bowl five times. In 1981, Winslow marked his second consecutive season leading the league in receptions—a first for a tight end—and was even chosen as the Pro Bowl Most Valuable Player, or MVP. In 1995, Winslow was voted into the Pro Football Hall of Fame. He is one of only seven tight ends, and only five Chargers, ever to receive that honor.

The Chicago Bears drafted Mike Ditka in 1961. Called Iron Mike, he was known for his great hands and his toughness. Ditka made himself known immediately in the NFL. In his first season, he scored 12 touchdowns, and he was named Rookie of the Year. Ditka's touchdown record stood until Antonio Gates scored 13 in 2004. Ditka went to five Pro Bowls and was named All-Pro three times, and he won a Super Bowl in 1972 as a member of the Dallas Cowboys. Ditka was later involved in two more Super Bowl victories: in 1974, as assistant coach of the Cowboys, and in 1985, as head coach of the Chicago Bears. Ditka made the Pro Football Hall of Fame in 1988, the first tight end ever to receive that honor. He later worked as head coach of the New Orleans Saints from 1997 to 2000, and he has also been a TV football commentator.

During Ditka's playing days, one of the other top tight ends was John Mackey. Like Ditka, Mackey was known for toughness and great hands. He played a total of ten seasons—nine with the Baltimore Colts and one with the San Diego Chargers. During that time (1963–1972), Mackey missed only one game. Mackey's 1966 season was especially impressive. Six of the nine touchdowns he scored that year covered 50 yards or more. After he retired, Mackey stayed in football as the president of the NFL Players Association. In 1992, Mackey became the second tight end to make the Pro Football Hall of Fame. (Go back to page 45.)

CHRONOLOGY

1980   Antonio Gates is born on June 18 in Detroit, Michigan.

1999   Antonio accepts a football scholarship to attend Michigan State University.

2002   In March, Antonio leads Kent State to the quarterfinals of the NCAA Division I men's basketball tournament.

2003   In August, the San Diego Chargers sign Antonio as an undrafted free agent.

2004   Antonio sets an NFL record for most touchdown catches by a tight end in a season, with 13.

2005   On January 8, Antonio sees his first playoff action and scores a touchdown in an overtime loss to the New York Jets.

        Antonio attends his first Pro Bowl on February 13 at Aloha Stadium in Honolulu, Hawaii.

        In late August, Antonio signs a six-year contract with the Chargers for an undisclosed amount.

2006   Antonio plays in his second consecutive Pro Bowl on February 12.

        The Chargers achieve a record of 14 wins and two losses, the best in franchise history.

2007   Antonio plays in his second playoff game on January 14, in which the Chargers lose to the New England Patriots.

        On February 10, Antonio plays in his third consecutive Pro Bowl.

2008   On January 6, Antonio dislocates his big toe in a playoff game against the Tennessee Titans.

        Antonio and the Chargers win two playoff games before losing to the New England Patriots in the AFC Championship game, 21-12.

        Antonio is selected for his fourth consecutive Pro Bowl.

        In late February, Antonio undergoes surgery for his injured toe and begins a lengthy recovery process.

ACCOMPLISHMENTS & AWARDS

Regular Season Career Statistics

Year	Team	Gms Pl	Gms St	Rec	Yds	Yds/R	Yds/G	Long	TD
2003	SD	15	11	24	389	16.2	25.9	48	2
2004	SD	15	15	81	964	11.9	64.3	72	13
2005	SD	15	15	89	1101	12.4	73.4	38	10
2006	SD	16	16	71	924	13.0	57.8	57	9
2007	SD	16	16	75	984	13.1	61.5	49	9
Career		77	73	340	4362	12.8	56.6		43

Postseason Career Statistics

Year	Team	Gms Pl	Gms St	Rec	Yds	Yds/R	Yds/G	Long	TD
2005	SD	1	1	6	89	14.8	89	44	1
2007	SD	1	1	6	61	10.2	61	19	0
2008	SD	3	3	6	60	10.0	20	23	0
Career		5	5	18	210	11.7	42.0		1

Personal Awards

- **1999** High School First-Team All-State in both football and basketball
- **2002** All-MAC power forward
  MAC champions
- **2003** All-MAC power forward
  Runner-up MAC Player of the Year
  Runner-up MAC champions
  All-America Honorable Mention
- **2005** NFL Pro Bowler
  NFL All-Pro
- **2006** NFL Pro Bowler
  NFL All-Pro
- **2007** NFL Pro Bowler
- **2008** NFL Pro Bowler

NFL Records Held

- **2004** Most Touchdowns scored by a tight end in a single season—13
- **2005** Most Touchdowns scored by a tight end in a two-year period—23 (2004, 2005)

Books and Periodicals

Chadiha, Jeffri. "The Tight End: Version 2.0." *Sports Illustrated* vol 105, no. 12 (September 25, 2006): p. 50-53.

Eisen, Rich. *Total Access: A Journey to the Center of the NFL Universe*. New York: Thomas Dunne Books, 2007.

Gramling, Gary. "In Good Hands." *Sports Illustrated for Kids* vol. 19, no. 11 (December 2007): p. G4-G8.

Hendricks, Sam. *Fantasy Football Guidebook*. College Station, TX: Virtualbookworm.com Publishing, 2007.

Leonetti, Mike, and John Laboni. *Football Now*. Richmond Hill, Ontario, Canada: Firefly Books, 2006.

Paolantonio, Sal, and Reuben Frank. *The Paolantonio Report: The Most Overrated and Underrated Players, Teams, Coaches, and Moments in NFL History*. Chicago: Triumph Books, 2007.

Web Sites

sports.espn.go.com/nfl/index
This site offers articles on just about everything to do with the NFL.

sports.espn.go.com/nfl/players/profile?statsId=6663
This site offers information on Antonio Gates's performance in individual games. You can also look up similar information about any player in the NFL.

www.chargers.com
This is the official site for the San Diego Chargers. It contains information about the team's schedule, players, and history, as well as its role in community events.

www.nflrush.com
This NFL Web site for kids features game, football news, and information about Play 60.

www.pro-football-reference.com
This Web site is very useful when looking for statistics and other information about NFL players, coaches, and teams, both past and present.

www.signonsandiego.com/sports/chargers/index.html
This is *The San Diego Union-Tribune's* online sports page about the San Diego Chargers. It contains detailed news about the team.

The Web sites mentioned in this book were active at the time of publication. The publisher is not responsible for Web sites that have changed their addresses or discontinued operation since the date of publication. The publisher will review and update the Web site addresses each time the book is reprinted.

GLOSSARY

Associated Press—a news organization that reports on many topics, including sports.

catch-and-run—a football play in which a player catches the ball, then runs for additional yards.

cornerback—a football player who defends against passes of more than five yards, usually covering the opposing team's wide receivers.

consecutive—in a row.

elude—to avoid skillfully.

extra-point kick—a kick, worth one point if the ball goes through the goalposts at the back of the end zone, that is attempted after a team scores a touchdown.

field goal—a kick, worth three points if the ball goes through the goalposts at the back of the end zone, that is generally attempted on fourth down.

fluke—an event that happens as a result of luck.

franchise—a term for a professional sports team and its operating organization.

hamper—to restrict the movement of something.

Huntington's disease—a genetic neurological disorder that causes problems with mental abilities, physical coordination, and behavior.

obesity—a condition in which a person's weight is more than 20 percent higher than is recommended for that person's height.

power forward—a player on a basketball team whose job it is to use size and strength to control the ball near the basket.

quarterback—the football player who directs the offensive play of his team.

scouts—people who observe prospective players and report to a team's management about the players' abilities.

snap—the act of starting a play by delivering the ball either to a quarterback, a holder, or another designated player.

stat line—the statistics accumulated by a player, coach, or team over the course of a game, season, or career.

touchdown—the act of scoring points by delivering the football into the opposing team's end zone, either by passing the ball or running with it. A touchdown itself is worth six points.

two-point conversion—two extra points earned after a touchdown if a team is able to run or pass the ball into the end zone from the two-yard line.

underdog—a team that is expected to lose in a struggle or contest, such as a sports event.

NOTES

page 6 "He has enough quickness . . ." Dan Pompei, "A Match Made for Gates? There Isn't One," *Sporting News* 229, no. 46 (November 18, 2005), p. 48.

page 7 "Antonio forces teams . . ." Jeffri Chadiha, "The Tight End: Version 2.0," *Sports Illustrated* 105, no. 12 (September 25, 2006), p. 50.

page 7 "He's actually kind of . . ." Gary Gramling, "In Good Hands," *Sports Illustrated for Kids* 19, no. 11 (December 2007), p. G4.

Page 9 "At the end of the year . . ." Antonio Gates, transcript of press conference, San Diego Chargers (November 10, 2004). http://www.chargers.com/news/headlines/news-110007360022489.htm.

page 10 "My family had the biggest . . ." Josh Staph, "Antonio Gates' Strength Training Plan," *Stack* (January 1, 2007). http://magazine.stack.com/TheIssue/Article/4082/Antonio_Antonio_Strength_Training_Plan.aspx.

page 12 "High school football in Detroit . . ." Marty Gitlin, "Player Spotlight: Antonio Gates," NFLHS.com (October 19, 2004). http://www.nflhs.com/news/playersspotlight/antoniogates_10192004_sim.asp

page 13 "I was young; seventeen . . ." Dave Hollander, "Chargers' Gates Says Revenge Not Goal," AOL.com (September 13, 2007). http://sports.aol.com/nfl/story/_a/chargers-Antonio-says-revenge-not-goal/20070911114409990001.

page 14 "Midway through my senior . . ." Gates, transcript of press conference.

page 15 "[T]he exposure I got . . ." Gitlin, "Player Spotlight: Antonio Gates."

page 17 "It became clear real fast . . ." Chadiha, "The Tight End: Version 2.0," p. 50.

page 21 "He was just feeling . . ." Jim Trotter, "A Bolt From the Blue," *Sporting News* 228, no. 40 (October 4, 2004), p. 44.

page 22 "In high school, every . . ." Gitlin, "Player Spotlight: Antonio Gates."

page 28 "I think I got Antonio . . ." Quoted in "Roundup: Gates Signs With Chargers for 'Gates Money'," *New York Times* (August 24, 2005). http://query.nytimes.com/gst/fullpage.html?res=950DEED6113EF937A1575BC0A9639C8B63&n=Top/News/Sports/Pro%20Football/National%20Football%20League/San%20Diego%20Chargers.

page 28 "The biggest key for . . ." Staph, "Antonio Gates' Strength Training Plan."

page 32 "The new-age tight end . . ." Chadiha, "The Tight End: Version 2.0," p. 50.

page 33 "I believe potential is . . ." Trotter, "A Bolt From the Blue," p. 44.

page 35 "I always anticipate going out . . ." Gates, transcript of press conference.

page 39 "He's more patient when . . ." Chadiha, "The Tight End: Version 2.0," p. 50

page 40 "It's one of those things . . ." Jon Robinson, "Antonio Gates Interview: Talking Madden, Chargers, and Rivers with the best tight end in the game," IGN.com (May 11, 2006). http://sports.ign.com/articles/708/708035p1.html.

NOTES

Page 40 "You pay the price for . . ." Antonio Gates "Play60" NFLRush.com (n.d.). http://www.nflrush.com/health/Antonio/5.

Page 41 "I haven't seen anyone . . ." Gramling, "In Good Hands," p. G4

page 43 "be the [number] 85 . . ." Antonio Gates, transcript of San Diego Chargers press conference (July 21, 2008). http://www.chargers.com/news/press-releases/press-release-2008072279917.php

page 45 "It's crazy how far . . . ." Quoted in "Antonio Gates: Progress Report on Toe Surgery," Rotowire.com (May 4, 2008). http://sports.yahoo.com/nfl/news?slug=rotowire-antonioatesrogressepo&prov=rotowire&type=fantasy.

page 45 "You never hear people say . . . ." Chadiha, "The Tight End: Version 2.0," p. 50.

INDEX

All-Pro Team, 51
American Football Conference (AFC), 46–47, 50–51
championship game, **43**

Bailey, Champ, 40–41, 51
basketball, 12–14, **15**, 48
Belichick, Bill, 6
Bolts. *See* San Diego Chargers
Brees, Drew, 7, 28, 30, 33

Central High School, 12–13
charity work, 39–40
Chrebet, Wayne, 49
Christensen, Todd, 25, 31
Clark, Dallas, 53
College of the Sequoias, 13
Colona, Andre, 27
contracts, NFL, 52
Crumpler, Alge, 53

Dearborn Community College, 13
Delhomme, Jake, 49
Ditka, Mike, 25, 55
draft, NFL, 49
Dungy, Tony, 50

Eastern Michigan University, 13

Faneca, Alan, 51
Farrior, James, **32**
Favre, Brett, 51
Flutie, Doug, **20**

Gates, Antonio
awards and honors won by, 13
and basketball, 12–14, **15**, 48
birth and childhood, 10–12
and celebrity, 33
and charity work, 39–40
and contract negotiations, 27–28
and earnings, 28
and family, 10
and grades, **11**, 13
in high school, 12–13
and injuries, **8**, 30, 42–44, 45
at Kent State University, 13–14, **15**, 48
on *Madden NFL* cover, 39
at Michigan State University, 13
and personal life, 33
and the playoffs, 25–26, **34**, 35, 42–43, 54
and the Pro Bowl, 8, 9, 25, 26, 30, **31**, 36, 42
rookie year, 16–21
is signed by the San Diego Chargers, 14–15
statistics, 8, 21, 25, 30–31
as tight end, 4–7, 9, 12–13, 17, 22, **32**, **37**, 45, 52, 55
See also San Diego Chargers
Gonzalez, Tony, **31**, 47, 52, 53

Hall, Dante, 24
Harrison, Marvin, 45
Holmes, Priest, 49

Johnson, Derrick, **29**
Jones, Walter, 51

Kent State University, 13–14, **15**, 48

Mackey, John, 55
Madden, John, 46
Madden NFL, 39
Manning, Peyton, 50
Manumaleuna, Brandon, 33
Matthews, Bruce, 47
Merriman, Shawne, 33
Michigan State University, 13
Moss, Randy, 45, 51

National Football Conference (NFC), 46–47, 50–51
National Football League (NFL), 46–47, 50–51
contracts, 52
draft, 49
Players Association, 52, 55
NCAA Championship tournament, 14, 48
NFL Play 60, 40
Nolan, Dick, 46

Oben, Roman, **7**
Olsen, Merlin, 47
Owens, Terrell, 51

Parker, Willie, 49
Pro Bowl, 8, 9, 25, 26, 30, **31**, 36, 42, 46–47

Qualcomm Stadium, 16, **17**

Reed, Ed, 51
Rice, Jerry, 51, 54
Rivers, Philip, 9, 33, 36, 39, 40–41, 42–43

Numbers in **bold italics** refer to captions.

INDEX

Saban, Nick, 13
San Diego Chargers, 4–8, 9
   2004 season, 21–22, 24–25
   2005 season, 28–31
   2006 season, 33–35, 54
   2007 season, 36–37, 39, 40–42
   and Gates's rookie year, 16–21
   history of, 54
   and the playoffs, 25–26, **34**, 35, 42–43, 54
   sign Gates, 14–15
      See also Gates, Antonio

Sanders, Barry, **31**
Sanders, James, **34**
Saturday, Jeff, 51
Schottenheimer, Marty, 16–17
Scott, Chad, **34**
Seau, Junior, 47
Smith, Jerry, 25
Smith, Rod, 49
Sports Illustrated for Kids, **38**, 39
Strahan, Michael, **31**
Super Bowl, 50–51, 54

"Take a Player to School" program, 40

tight ends, 4, **5**, 6–7, 9, 22, 25, 31, **32**, **37**, 46, 52–53, 55
Tomlinson, LaDainian, 9, 19, 21, 22, **23**, 25, 28, 33, 35, 39, 40, 42, 51, 54

Walls, Wesley, 25
Warner, Kurt, 49
Welker, Wes, 49
Williams, Kevin, 51
Winslow, Kellen, Jr., 53
Winslow, Kellen, Sr., 55
Witten, Jason, 53

Young, Steve, 54

ABOUT THE AUTHOR

Ian Kimmich is the author of a novel, numerous short stories, and a book for young readers about Steve Nash. He is also a book editor and lives in Portland, Oregon.

PICTURE CREDITS

page

- **5:** George Bridges/KRT
- **7:** Contra Costa Times/MCT
- **8:** Zack Everson/SPCS
- **11:** San Diego Magazine/NMI
- **12:** Robin Adams/SPCS
- **15:** Jon Ridinger/SPCS
- **17:** T&T/IOA Photos
- **18:** Scott Gould/SPCS
- **20:** SportChrome Pix
- **23:** Sports Illustrated/NMI
- **24:** Joe Ledford/Kansas City Star/KRT
- **27:** Lisa Blumenfeld/Getty Images
- **29:** Kansas City Star/KRT
- **31:** beejayreyes/AASI Photos
- **32:** Scott Gould/SPCS
- **34:** StreetLampProductions/AASI Photos
- **37:** SportChrome Pix
- **38:** Sports Illustrated/NMI
- **41:** Chicago Tribune/MCT
- **43:** Eric Yeaton/AASI Photos
- **44:** Scott Gould/SPCS
- **47:** Zack Everson/SPCS
- **49:** Sports Illustrated/NMI
- **50:** Joe Rimkus Jr./Miami Herald/MCT
- **53:** AP Photo/Charlie Reidel
- **54:** NFL/PRMS

Front cover: Contra Costa Times/MCT
Front cover inset: Scott Gould/SPCS